Memory Journal - Dino Edition
Copyright 2019
All Rights Reserved

This Memory Journal was crafted with love for:

Always be yourself unless you can be a dinosaur - then always be a dinosaur!

You make me feel roarsome!

ROARR

EASTER

COLORING EGGS

EGG
CHOCOLATE
HUNT
Jelly Beans
Hippity Hoppity PEEPS

Blossom

April Showers

SPRING   Daffodils

Sunshine

Bees

Butterflies

Tulips

MAYFLOWERS

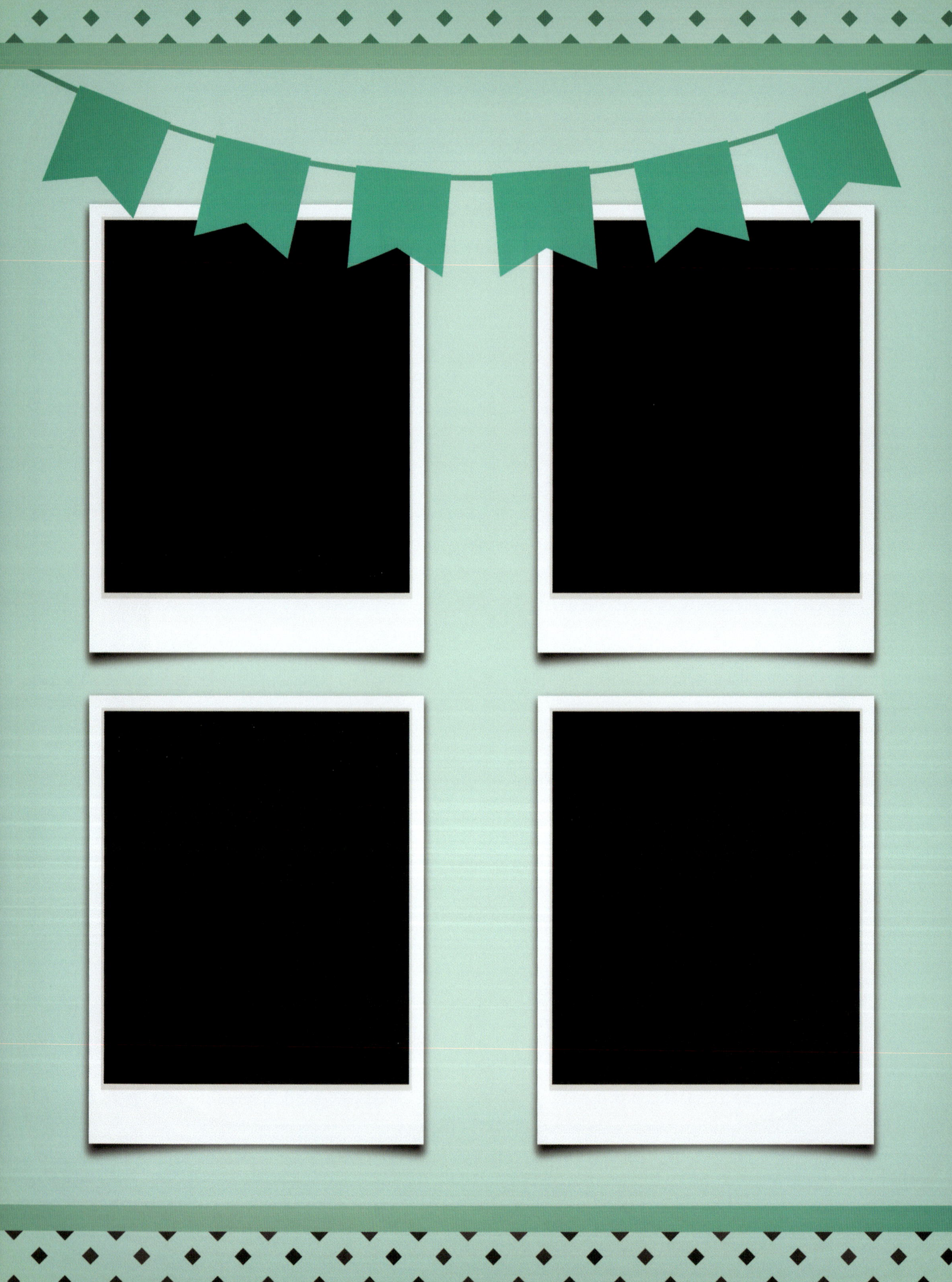

FAMILY Beach swimming

sleeping under SUMMER FUN

the stars BBQ

-EVERY-
summer
HAS a
story

bonfires CAMPING

ride the waves relax

I'ts Your
Birthday!

So many of my smiles start with you...

GRRR
RAWR
GRRR

Fall Fun!

Let
it
Snow

Printed in Great Britain
by Amazon